101
Ways to
Stop Shopping
and
Start Saving

KRISSY FALZON

Cover illustration by Frank Falzon

ISBN: 1456558021
ISBN-13: 9781456558024

INTRODUCTION

Are you a compulsive shopper? Do you run to the store to pick up paper towels and shaving cream but come home with bags of stuff? Are you accumulating clutter because you can't stop shopping? *101 Ways to Stop Shopping and Start Saving* will make you think twice before you decide to walk into the next store.

Get 101 ideas including how to:

- resist the temptation to shop and spend money
- put "retail therapy" in perspective
- understand the importance of a budget
- pay down debt & start saving
- Track spending with included Cash Record Sheets

Take the first step to help yourself curb the urge to shop by following the tips outlined in this fun and easy to read book!

1 The first step to help you resist shopping is to decide on a future goal you would like to save for. It could be a house, a trip, a car, etc. Make it something you are passionate about. Set up an account or even a simple envelope marked for this special savings goal. Determine how much you would need to save. When you go into stores you need to remember this goal and ask yourself if whatever you are planning on buying is worth deducting money out of that account.

2 Find your weak spots and remove temptations. Cancel mail order catalogs, stay out of all stores, and block channels on your television if you purchase from the tube. Can't stop online shopping? Post a neon sticky note that says "No More Shopping" near your computer with a picture of your goal to serve as a visual reminder.

3 What do you say to yourself when you are buying something you shouldn't be? Think about your answers. Do you tell yourself, "I deserve it!"? Maybe you do, but you also deserve to stay disciplined so you can reach your goals. You must realize that each little purchase, no matter how small or insignificant, is taking away savings from your real goal.

4 Make a list <u>prior</u> to shopping; take it with you and STICK TO YOUR LIST. Do not buy anything that is not on the list (unless you NEED it).

Stop buying random things. A candy bar, a pretty note cube, etc. – do you really *need* those things? Is that what you went in the store to buy? Stick to your list and avoid impulse purchases.

5 If you were to add up all of your credit card statements for the last few years, what would they total?

You will see just how much money you could have saved. Do you even remember what you bought with all of those charges? Was it worth it?

This will help you realize how small charges over time add up to large sums of money. Think twice before you buy.

6 When you go into a store, make it your mission to go in and get out <u>as quickly as possible</u>. Stick to your list and buy only what is on the list, which is what you <u>need</u>.

Do not wander through the mall or stores to pass time as you will inevitably see things you want. Why tempt yourself? Stay out of stores as much as possible.

7 YOU can change your shopping and spending habits right now. YOU ARE IN CONTROL of your spending. It is up to you to make wise choices with your money.

8 DON'T TOUCH OR PICK UP ITEMS IN STORES. Many times you become attached to the item. What happens when you pick up a sweater, then you put it down, but then someone else walks over and picks it up? You probably feel anxious and say to yourself – "Hey -get off that! It's mine!" So don't touch anything – just look.

9 Don't sell yourself products. How many times have you talked yourself into "needing" something? You see an apple-peeling machine. You tell yourself, "I could see myself using this for baking an apple pie." Then you create a scenario in your mind and you see yourself using the product. Stop selling *to yourself.*

10

Talk yourself out of buying things. Say the following words – "I don't need that." It is a powerful statement to make and it will help you to pause and decide not to buy.

11

You have to realize the designers, stores and salespeople are out to make money. The stores want to sell their clothes, accessories, shoes, etc. <u>to make money.</u> They paid a lot less money for their inventory than what they're charging YOU. They have to pay for the overhead of running their store – rent, electric, employee costs (salary, benefits) – you get the idea. The designers are hoping you'll get sucked into the idea of branding and fancy marketing ploys. Don't be fooled.

When you shop, look for quality and comfort. Just because something costs hundreds or thousands of dollars doesn't mean it's any better than a less expensive copy. Would you rather make *them* richer or have more money in YOUR account? Be smart with your hard-earned money!

12 Stop shopping like a zombie and ask yourself the following questions before buying something:

13
Do I *need* this or do I *want* this? Don't confuse needs with wants. Examples of needs are: shelter, food, water, and clothes. Another pair of designer shoes is not a "need," it's a want. If you are trying to curb your shopping and start saving, then you need to distinguish between the two. You can do it!

14

How long have I wanted this? Is this an impulse purchase?

How many times have you bought a gorgeous pair of shoes or an outfit although you weren't really planning on it? Then you see the charge a month later and regret it. That's an impulse purchase. On the road to saving money, you cannot make impulse purchases. If you want to buy something, pay cash for it or save for it like they did in the old days.

15 Can I afford this?

Many people who use credit cards forgo asking themselves this simple question. Be honest with yourself. Can you really afford this item? If you cannot pay off the charge in full, no, you cannot afford it. How many work hours did it cost for you to buy it? Would it be worth two working days? Think about this before buying things.

16

Where will I put this?

Do you really have the room? If we all bought *everything* we liked we would need a warehouse to store everything. If you do not have a specific place for something, *it is clutter*. The item will end up in a catch-all room, like a basement or spare room – and eventually, a yard sale.

17 What else can I get for this money? When you are about to spend money, you should ask yourself, "What else can I use this money for that I really need?" A new washing machine? A new pair of eyeglasses?

18 Why am I buying this? Do I think I'll impress someone? Am I trying to keep up with other people? Am I bored?

Don't buy something to keep up with other people. You are not in a race so go at your own pace and buy things you can afford. Dress up your old outfits with new accessories. When your bank account gets larger you'll be happy you didn't spend all your money on *things*!

If you are shopping because you are bored, recognize that and do something about it. Take a walk with a friend instead or volunteer at a local animal shelter. If you're bored, shopping will only be a *temporary* fix.

19

Take note of key triggers that tempt you to overspend.

For example, many people get excited over the holidays and spend much more than originally planned.

Does this sound like you? If so, write a gift list and set a budget. Stick to your list to avoid overspending.

20 Pursue your passion – spend time doing what you enjoy. If you don't know what your passion is, what is the one thing you love to do and lose track of time (hours pass and it felt like minutes)? Spend time doing what you love and have fun (out of stores!).

21 Will this end up in a future yard sale or will I really use this?

What have you seen at garage sales? People's things they are no longer using or never even used. If you don't love whatever you're buying and if you don't really need it, odds are it will end up in your next yard sale. Only buy things you love and need.

22 You don't have to buy everything you like. Everything admired doesn't have to be acquired! Or remember this shorter saying: Admire it, not acquire it. Don't add to any clutter you may already have.

23 Look around your home. Imagine if you could get cash for everything you have and aren't using. Wouldn't you like that extra cash? It could probably add up to thousands! Think about this before you go to the store and buy more things.

24 Invest in better quality accessories, such as handbags, watches, and jewelry. Tip: Instead of wearing a few fashion watches, buy a timeless (no pun intended) piece and make that your signature watch. You will be truly happy with what you are wearing and you won't have any reason to keep shopping for watches or handbags. Hopefully you'll be satisfied with what you already own.

25 Makeup collectors: Try using your makeup until it is finished before buying new makeup (stay within expiration dates). How many years will it take you to finish all of your shadows, blushes, etc.? Unused makeup is wasted money.

26 Clean out your clothes closet! Donate any clothes that no longer fit you, aren't comfortable, and don't "do something" for you. Organize your clothes by category and hang them on extra-thin hangers to create more space in your closet. You'll be happier with your new space and know what you have so you don't buy clothes you don't need.

27 Be prepared on-the-go and save money.

When you are out for the day, be prepared so you don't have to spend extra cash. Carry a hooded sweatshirt, beverages, a snack or lunches, medicine, a spare shirt – anything you might need. Buying bottled water for you and your family can quickly add up. If you get chilly while strolling on the boardwalk, you won't have to buy something to stay warm. Anticipate possible needs to save money.

28 Learn to live with less. Accept that what you ALREADY HAVE is ENOUGH. Appreciate what you have now.

De-clutter your home and you will be able to think more clearly. When you keep shopping and don't follow the standard "one-in-one-out" rule, your purchases will accumulate and take up valuable space.

29 Keep what you earn. Stop making *everyone else* rich. Save your hard-earned money and let it build each week. You'll be so much happier for it!

30 Where do you pay your bills? Your desk should be neat and clutter-free for handling your finances. You need to think clearly and effectively. Keep only necessary items on your desk: a calculator, checkbook, a pen and pencil, a highlighter, stapler, stamps and return address labels. Display a picture of your goal to help you stay motivated.

31
If I am charging this, will I be able to pay the bill in full when it's due? Get out of the habit of making charges. If you can't pay the bill in full that means you cannot afford it. It's very simple. It means NO. Try to tell yourself "no" to charging and listen to yourself! Everyone is used to charging whatever they want because they don't feel the cash coming out of their pockets. Stop this habit as soon as possible by paying only in cash.

32   Although your debit card deducts cash from your account, and you're not racking up credit card charges, you are still not "feeling" the cash being taken out of your wallet. You don't see the actual money disappear. Try to only pay with cash.

33 Resist sales: Just because you're getting a "deal" doesn't mean you should buy it. If you don't have the space for whatever you are buying it is actually costing you in valuable real estate space.

34 How many clothes do you have with tags still attached? If you aren't wearing them, sell them if possible. If you can't sell them, then chalk it up to a lesson learned – bargains aren't always worth it. If you don't love the outfit, you're not going to wear it. Donate it and free space in your closet. It might have been a bargain, but it is actually costing you in space.

35 Think about how many hours of work would equal the cost of the item. If you buy a handbag for $100 and you make $10 an hour, it would take you 10 work hours to earn that bag. Is it worth it? A dollar saved is a dollar earned.

36 *Where* you shop can influence *what* you buy. For example: If you are in a shop on Fifth Avenue, ask yourself: "If I saw this same item at A-Z Discount Mart, would I still want it?" The answer would probably be "no," as the item became less appealing. This puts things in perspective, doesn't it? The excitement of *where* we are shopping can disillusion us all. Use this tactic when shopping on vacations, too!

37

Don't shop when you are not feeling well. You are apt to buy things you don't need just to lift your mood. Remember, it's only temporary.

38 Do you receive packages at home but can't remember what you ordered? What does that tell you? You don't really NEED what you ordered. If you did, you'd be missing the item every day.

39 You may feel you deserve all the things you want, but don't you deserve to be debt-free? Look at the big picture: remember all of the credit card statements you had over the years and could not even recall what was purchased. Keep this in your mind to curb the urge to shop. Look at the big picture and remember all of the credit card statements you had over the years and couldn't even remember what you bought.

40 Collections: Are you a collector? Do you really NEED to collect more makeup, perfume, handbags, shoes, knick-knacks, etc.? How many shoes do you really NEED? How many handbags will you ever really use?

Now is the time to change. As I said earlier, enjoy what you already have. Collections can quickly take up valuable space in your home. Decide on a specific number and donate or sell the rest. If your collections end up in a pile of clutter, you won't be able to appreciate them.

41 Before you buy something ask yourself, "Is this worth a) taking money from my future goals/saving account, b) adding to my credit card debt, c) paying more money for this item later on with accrued finance charges?"

42 Watch out for impulse buys: Items are strategically placed at store registers for people to make impulse purchases. Before you put something else in your cart, ask yourself the following questions:

1) "Can I wait to buy this item?"
2) "Is this an impulse purchase or was it on my list?"
3) "Do I <u>need</u> this?"
4) "*Why* do I want to buy this?"

☙❧

43

Streamline your jewelry and perfume collections. Keep only a few and make them your signature pieces.

44 Wait to make large purchases. Can this wait until next week? Wait a week and then if you remember the item and you will use it because you need it, buy it with cash.

Do your research and shop around for the lowest price on large ticket items. If you are buying online, always look for a "promo code" or "coupon code" to reduce costs.

45 Why are you shopping? If you keep buying WANTS, ask yourself WHY? Do you feel upset? Are you trying to fill a void with things? Try filling your life with experiences. Spend time with friends, family, working or traveling, etc. Help others and you'll feel amazing.

46 If you look back years from now and see all of the thousands of dollars you spent on "who knows what," knowing that you could have had that money in a savings account, how will you feel? Stop shopping and spending your money on things you don't need.

47 Clear out your clutter and see what you already have. Do you need a black pair of pants or do you have 5 pairs? Write a list of things you NEED. If you can actually see what is in your closet, you won't make senseless purchases.

48 Contribute to a retirement plan. If your job offers to match your contribution, take advantage of that. If not, you can open a retirement account on your own. Be sure to save as much as you can comfortably afford. (Don't forget to save for your emergency fund, too!)

49 Create a budget. Be aware of how much you are spending and on what. You need to know how much money is coming in and how much is going out.

Also, know what you owe:

Gather all of your credit card statements and call each of the companies to find out the current total balance that you owe. Make a commitment to yourself to change your spending habits TODAY.

50 Set limits on spending. Train yourself to stick to a budget. If you only allow yourself $60 a week on eating out, don't go over that amount. Write the amount and what the money is for on the outside of envelopes. When the money is gone – it's gone! Sorry, no more spending! You could also staple a sticky note to the cash. On the sticky note you would write what the money is for and the allotted amount. For example: "$30 - Entertainment." The staple will also help you think twice before taking the cash for something else.

51

Track your daily spending with the Cash Record Sheets in the back of this book. The Cash Record Sheets have columns and lines for adding up totals.

Each day, write down EVERY item you buy. If you buy a coffee for $1, write that down.

Each week, take a look at your spending habits so you can see where your money is going. You will be able to see which area(s) you need to cut back on.

52 Reward yourself with an experience for every month of not spending money on things you don't need. You can go out to eat, get your nails done, go to the movies, etc. Don't accumulate things you don't need and won't use.

53 Sign up for an automatic savings plan. Each month set aside a certain amount of money for future goals. It is vital to your financial success to have a goal in mind. You need to keep this goal in your mind to stop shopping and spending money that could otherwise be going into the savings account for your special goal.

54 Respect your money. Keep your handbag and wallet neat and free of junk papers. Your cash should be in order and neatly arranged. Stash a $50 or $100 bill in a hidden slot in your wallet for emergencies. Your wallet should be one you love and are proud to use. The idea here is to create positive energy surrounding your finances.

55 Get new things for free! Have a handbag exchange party. Invite a few friends over and everyone can leave with a "new" handbag to enjoy. (you can do this with other things such as video games, books, magazines, etc.). This is another option to avoid spending to get "new" things.

56

If you saved money to go away on vacation, always set a budget first. Before you go on vacation, decide how much money you will need for everything such as: food, gas, tolls, hotel, hotel tips, amusement park tickets, and souvenirs (one per person!). It is better to *overestimate* so you will not end up short.

For example: Place the allotted amount of cash in an envelope labeled "Food - $200", etc.. If you will be away for 4 nights, you will need enough money for 4 dinners out. Let's assume that each dinner will cost approximately $50 for two people. You will need to set aside $200 ($50 x 4 dinners) in an envelope.

Remember Tip # 27 and be prepared while away to save money!

57 Plan for upcoming events. Save money ahead of time for monetary gifts for weddings, birthdays, holidays, etc. This way you'll be able to stick to your budget.

58 Enroll in a holiday savings club. Each holiday season you will be ready to shop *with cash*. You will also start the new year off without incurring any debt. (Remember to write your gift list and stick to your budget!).

59 How many things have you thrown out because you were no longer using them? Think about that before you buy something and bring it into your home.

60 Treasure hunter? Stop going to garage sales. There are so many cheap things, people tend to overbuy and then clutter their own homes. Don't pull over – keep driving.

61 Make a game of saving money. Try to go each day with spending either nothing or $5 maximum.

62 Each day bring lunch to work. If you can't imagine doing that, try it for a few days. $6 a day on lunch will save you $30 in a week or $120 a month! $1440 a year! What would you want to buy for $1440? Keep it in an account and next year you'll have almost $3,000 to spend! What would you rather have? Lunches out or $3,000?

63
Have a garage sale every so often. Start making money on things you no longer use. Deposit this money into a savings account.

64 Set up a savings account for a specific goal. If you are saving for a trip to Europe, open an account and save each month for your goal.

65 Before you take that cash out of your wallet, imagine your savings account for your goal *decreasing* in value.

66 Get another job if possible to bring in more cash flow. Put your skills to use. If you have makeup skills, babysitting, etc. – do what you can to make money.

67

Make it a game: Try to go without buying anything but the basic necessities.

68 Get your haircut at a less expensive hair salon or go to a beauty school for steep discounts.

69 Save for a 3-6 month emergency fund (a year is even better!). This means you should have enough money to cover at least 3-6 months of expenses.

70

If you enjoy shopping, consider starting your own shopping business. Shop for other people and get paid for it!

71

Each time you pay with cash, don't use coins. Get change back from every transaction. Go home and deposit those coins into a jar with a wide mouth, so it's quick and easy. Before you know it you'll have saved a nice chunk of change! Cash it in and add it to your special savings account.

72 Keep track of what you are buying and the running total, whether it is for clothes or food. TIP: Many supermarkets have portable scanners that you take with you while you shop. You scan the items yourself and the scanner displays the running total.

73 Pay off credit card debt. You are wasting money paying monthly finance charges.

Where else could that money be used? Wouldn't you like to see it added to your savings account?

74 Pay more than the minimum on credit cards each month. Pay the card with the highest interest rate first or if it motivates you, pay off one in full and then move to the next one.

75

Have parties at your place instead of paying expensive restaurant and bar costs.

Invite friends over and enjoy conversations, play games or watch a movie. You can ask everyone to bring a snack and drinks.

76 Identify what you splurge on the most. Is it going out to eat twice a week for $100? Go out once a month instead. Get take-out and bring it home or eat it in the restaurant for some type of dining experience. It might not be fancy waitress service, but so what? You're out – have fun!

77

As I mentioned earlier, purchasing food out is costly. Bring leftovers from last night's dinner to eat for lunch.

So many people spend upwards of $8 a day on lunch. Do you realize how much they could be saving? $40.00 per week, which is $160 a month! And $1,920.00 per year! $19,200 over 10 years! That's almost TWENTY THOUSAND DOLLARS SAVED just from not spending $8 on lunches!

78

Make your coffee at home. If you spend $2 a day on a cup of coffee, that amounts to $10 a week or $40 a month or $480 a year – on a drink! In 4 years, that's almost $2,000 – on coffee! And $4,800 in 10 years! That puts things in perspective, doesn't it?

79

Now combine that savings from bringing your own lunch and coffee ($4,800 + $19,200) and you will have a whopping $24,000 in 10 years!!! So you see where you can save with just a small change. What would you do with that extra money?

80 Read the supermarket circulars and create a menu around what food is on sale that week. Use coupons at stores that double the savings.

81 Cook larger meals and freeze them. For example: Make two trays of baked ziti and freeze one for a couple weeks from now.

Stretch your meals by serving them with rice, vegetables and/or salad.

82 Love to read magazines? Swap them with your friends or take them out from your local library for free. Some people pay $20 a month or more for their magazine habit! That is $240 a year or $2,400 in ten years! (on magazines?!!).

83 Don't grocery shop when you are hungry – you'll be tempted to buy things that are not on your list.

84
Clear the clutter out of your house and sell or consign items you no longer use. Have a yard sale or sell your items online. Having a clutter-free home will help you to focus and think more clearly.

85

Pay your credit card bill in full each month. Don't pay more money for things you already charged. Get in the habit of paying off your cards in full every month. (but please, try to pay cash for everything you can!)

86 Do you get *weekly* manicures? How much do they cost? Let's assume the price of a manicure is $6 and you give $1.50 for a tip. This totals $30 a month or $360 a year or $1,800 in 5 years!

Save money by polishing your nails at home. Purchase a manicure kit: quality nail enamel, base coat, top coat, files, nail clippers, etc.. Even if you have to spend $20, you will save hundreds *or thousands* of dollars in the long term. You could also request a gift certificate to your nail salon for your birthday or the holidays.

87

Wean yourself off of expensive designer names. Do most people know it's that certain designer? Does it really matter? Look for quality when you are shopping. Just because there is a designer label doesn't necessarily mean the article of clothing is the best quality for the money. In most cases you are paying FOR the name.

88 If you are bored, do not go shopping. Watch TV, go out with a friend, exercise, do something other than shopping! Shopping is a temporary fix so it is important that you find another activity you enjoy.

❧❧

89

Leave your credit cards at home or carry them for emergencies, but secure them in an envelope that is marked "for emergencies only" and tape it up and seal it very well.

90

Shop from your own closet! Create new outfits with accessories such as scarves, pins and jewelry.

Swap clothes with a friend and you will both have something new to wear!

Why spend money on new clothes if you don't have to?

91
Whatever you don't buy for yourself you can suggest as gift ideas for family and friends to buy you for your birthday or the holidays.

92 Don't hire people for work you can do yourself. If you can mow the lawn, paint your house, etc.. – do it yourself and keep the savings.

93 Shopping on your lunch hour? Instead, play a game of chess with co-workers or take a walk in the park.

❧

94

When you get the Sunday paper, don't even look at the sale ads. Ignore them.

Out of sight – out of mind.

95
Only clip coupons for items you use. Otherwise you'll just end up buying things that your family doesn't use.

96 Don't put off what you can start today – start saving! Even if it's only the change in your pocket – it's something! Remember, the less you spend, the more you save.

97

Don't put anything in your shopping cart unless you are definitely buying it. If you put all the extra things in your cart that you "aren't sure about" you will most likely end up purchasing them. This is for both in the store and online.

98

Buy better quality when possible – in most cases the item will last longer and you'll probably be happier with your purchases.

99 Salespeople want you to think everything they're selling is great. Maybe it is, but if you don't need it, you have to ignore sales pitches.

100

Instead of buying something you don't need, imagine if you donated that amount to save lives at animal shelters or *any* charity you would like to help. They could put the money to good use. Now, how appealing is that handbag?

101

Pay down any loans you have. Homeowners: If you have a mortgage, pay extra to the principal of your mortgage. You'll save thousands in the long run.

❧

The following pages contain Bonus tips and Cash Record Sheets so you can track your spending.

102

Are you shopping because it makes you happy? Understand it is a temporary fix and when it goes away you'll be back out at the mall shopping.

103

When you receive money for birthdays or holidays, place it in an envelope marked, "Birthday/Holiday Money." Over the year, if there is something you really want to buy, use the cash in this envelope to pay for it.

104 Save your money and value yourself – not things.

For example, carrying an expensive designer purse might make you feel happy, but it just means you paid *a lot more money* for a bag and you have *that much less* in your savings account. What you own does not define who you are.

105 You will get motivated and excited to watch your savings grow each month.

106

If your salary is $30,000 a year, you will have earned $300,000 in ten years. We know how much goes to taxes and expenses, but just imagine how much you could save if you stopped buying unnecessary things.

107

Carry emergency cash with you at all times. Keep a $50 or $100 bill in a hidden slot in your wallet. This will safeguard you from using your credit card in an emergency.

108 Imagine how free you will feel when you don't have any credit cards to pay.

109 Maintain orderly files for your bank statements, checking and savings registers.

110

Be proud of reading this book and beginning your journey to curbing your urge to shop and starting to save!

❦

❦

Remember, the best things in life are FREE!

❦

❦❦❦❦❦❦❦❦❦❦❦❦❦❦❦❦❦

HOW TO USE THE CASH RECORD SHEETS

Use the following pages to keep track of your daily spending.
Record everything you buy, even if it's a purchase for 50 cents.

To help track your spending on needs and wants, you may write "N" for Need, "W" for Want, under the "Reason for Purchase" column. At the end of each day, total the amount spent. Within a few weeks you will be able to see just where your money is going.

Take control of your spending - you can do it!

See sample below:

DATE	ITEM PURCHASED	REASON FOR PURCHASE	TOTAL
7/1/17	Coffee	W	1.75
7/1/17	Tip at Coffee Shop	W	.50
7/1/17	Vegetables	N	7.58
7/1/17		TOTAL SPENT:	9.83

CASH RECORD SHEET

DATE	ITEM PURCHASED	REASON FOR PURCHASE	TOTAL SPENT

CASH RECORD SHEET

DATE	ITEM PURCHASED	REASON FOR PURCHASE	TOTAL SPENT

CASH RECORD SHEET

DATE	ITEM PURCHASED	REASON FOR PURCHASE	TOTAL SPENT

CASH RECORD SHEET

DATE	ITEM PURCHASED	REASON FOR PURCHASE	TOTAL SPENT

CASH RECORD SHEET

DATE	ITEM PURCHASED	REASON FOR PURCHASE	TOTAL SPENT

CASH RECORD SHEET

DATE	ITEM PURCHASED	REASON FOR PURCHASE	TOTAL SPENT

CASH RECORD SHEET

DATE	ITEM PURCHASED	REASON FOR PURCHASE	TOTAL SPENT

CASH RECORD SHEET

DATE	ITEM PURCHASED	REASON FOR PURCHASE	TOTAL SPENT

CASH RECORD SHEET

DATE	ITEM PURCHASED	REASON FOR PURCHASE	TOTAL SPENT

CASH RECORD SHEET

DATE	ITEM PURCHASED	REASON FOR PURCHASE	TOTAL SPENT

CASH RECORD SHEET

DATE	ITEM PURCHASED	REASON FOR PURCHASE	TOTAL SPENT

CASH RECORD SHEET

DATE	ITEM PURCHASED	REASON FOR PURCHASE	TOTAL SPENT

CASH RECORD SHEET

DATE	ITEM PURCHASED	REASON FOR PURCHASE	TOTAL SPENT

CASH RECORD SHEET

DATE	ITEM PURCHASED	REASON FOR PURCHASE	TOTAL SPENT

CASH RECORD SHEET

DATE	ITEM PURCHASED	REASON FOR PURCHASE	TOTAL SPENT

CASH RECORD SHEET

DATE	ITEM PURCHASED	REASON FOR PURCHASE	TOTAL SPENT

CASH RECORD SHEET

DATE	ITEM PURCHASED	REASON FOR PURCHASE	TOTAL SPENT

CASH RECORD SHEET

DATE	ITEM PURCHASED	REASON FOR PURCHASE	TOTAL SPENT

CASH RECORD SHEET

DATE	ITEM PURCHASED	REASON FOR PURCHASE	TOTAL SPENT

CASH RECORD SHEET

DATE	ITEM PURCHASED	REASON FOR PURCHASE	TOTAL SPENT

CASH RECORD SHEET

DATE	ITEM PURCHASED	REASON FOR PURCHASE	TOTAL SPENT